B I P O L A R

An Unorthodox, Common Sense Explanation

by Jay Carter, Psy.D.

Unicorn Press
PO Box 6048
Wyomissing, PA 19610

Graphics by Corel WordPerfect Vers. 5.1 & 6.0

This publication is meant to provide accurate and authoritative information in regard to the subject matter covered according to the references and personal experience of the author. The author is not a medical doctor or psychiatrist and the publication is not meant to substitute for such. Always consult a physician about these matters. If assistance is required, consult a medically trained professional. Some of the content in this publication is based upon the phenomenological observance of the author and has not been scientifically proven. But if it looks like a rose, smells like a rose, and feels like a rose ... it's probably a rose. Science is limited. The human spirit is undefinable in the context of science and must be phenomenologically explained with unscientific things like ... compassion ... love ... caring ... humor. By the same token, the bipolar disorder must be explained the same way, in addition to scientific explanations.

Every effort was made, phenomenologically, to make sure the information in this book is correct, which means ... it is MOSTLY right. If this book were likened to a drug, it shows a great deal of promise ... but is not yet FDA approved. Mostly, the information in this book helps someone put the bipolar disorder into perspective, and that is the greatest value. Most other books are only mostly right too. They just don't usually admit it.

ISBN 0-937004-16-2
Third Edition
Third Printing
Now More pages
More information

God, give me the serenity to accept the things I cannot change, the courage to change the things I can, and the wisdom to know the difference.

Acknowledgements

Special thanks to the psychiatrists, medical doctors, psychologists, nurses, social workers, and counselors across the country attending my seminars who contributed phenomenological information to this book. Thanks to Dr. Michelle Munson who the first reader and who gave me objective feedback and to Dr. Loretta Martin-Halpine. Thanks to Sharon Wright. Appreciation to Sue Bray at Bookmasters who helps to keep the price down on this book. Thanks to my mother and daughter for being who they are.

This is what people have said about this book:

"Fantastic! It is good to know the phenomenological feedback from the nurses and therapists in the trenches" (psychiatrist)

"Less ... is so much more!" (psychologist)

"Such a compassionate book." (social worker)

"Such a fresh new perspective. Enlightening, professionally and personally." (psychologist)

"I understand it for the first time in 30 years." (a counselor who is bipolar)

"Dr. Jay thinks out of the box, but this is right on the money." (social worker)

"This book got me in my prefrontal lobe. I am giving a copy to all my bipolar clients." (psychologist)

"I feel so relieved." (bipolar mother of a bipolar child)

Dedicated to my mother and other bipolar butterflies with tattered wings.

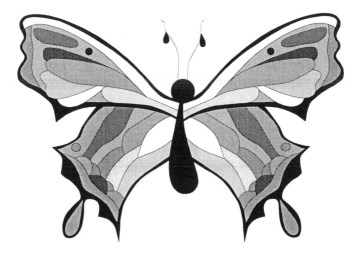

Table of Contents

From the Author ... 9

Introduction ... 11

The Psychiatric "Bible" ... 21

Bipolar Stories ... 31
    The Lord
    The Bank Robber
    Sarah
    Billy The Kid
    One Time Forgiveness
    The Business Addict
    Bipolar Kids

Bipolar Kids ... 43

Balancing ... 47
    Self Medication
    Psychotropic Medication
    Bio-feedback

Reasonable Explanations ... 55
    Intervening
    Evolution
    Research and Other Things
    The Spirit
Suggested Readings
Bibliography

From the Author

First of all, if you do not have a sense of humor, do not purchase this book. This is an unorthodox, common sense, non-technical approach to the bipolar subject with a sense of humor. This is not a cavalier approach as you will realize by the end of the book. I realize that some bipolars have serious problems, but I have found that most bipolars have a good sense of humor. Most bipolars also "think out of the box." So, this book has a sense of humor and it "thinks out of the box." I wrote it for bipolars. I am respectful when I talk about <u>bipolars</u> vs. the bipolar disorder. I believe that there is a bipolar temperament and when this temperament gets awry, we call it the bipolar disorder.

This is not a scientific book. Oh sure, I have all the credentials necessary to write a technical book on the subject and this could be "yet another book on the bipolar disorder." Ah! I'd rather stick pins in my eye than do that.

In my lectures, seminars, and one-on-one evaluations, I have found that there are not too many people who understand the bipolar problem on a common sense basis. Many people take medication without really understanding much about it. They might know that it is for a chemical and heredity problem, and they know what effect it has on them from their own experience, but that's all. Most people only spend fifteen minutes, or so, with their psychiatrist, and after the initial evaluation, are treated medically. He/she is, first, a physician. Fifty percent of people who are bipolar are unhappy with the amount of doctor time they get. Medical doctors are there to assess them ... medically, and managed care does not pay for the doctor to spend a lot of time talking to a patient. That would be the therapist's job.

You wanna hear about my credentials? Yes, I know you are so excited. Well, I need to tell you anyway. I am a licensed psychologist. I have a Certification in Psychoactive Substance Abuse Disorders by the American Psychological Association (APA). I am a Candidate Diplomate in Psychopharmacology educated in a program sanctioned by the APA. I am also a Diplomate Forensic Psychologist. But, most of all, I was raised as a farmer. Things have to make common sense. I have learned a lot from doing over 6000 evaluations, being educated, and being around experienced people, but this book is written mostly from my farmer perspective.

I see the bipolar aspect through four windows:
 1. My personal experience in family
relationships.
 2. Observing the effects of medication on
people with the bipolar disorder.
 3. Six years experience at a rehab.
 4. A forensic perspective from two and a half
years as a psychologist at a prison.

I hope I have saved you time and effort by reducing this book into a palatable amount of information. Sometimes less is more.

INTRODUCTION

The latest understanding of the bipolar disorder is that it is a genetic and chemical disorder. It was called Manic-Depression, but it has been found to be more of a medical problem than a psychological problem, even though people may act crazy who have the disorder. Guess what it was called before "Manic-Depression"? It was called the cyclothymic personality disorder. And that's why I have a hard time believing in "personality disorders". (Cause bipolar isn't one ... and it wasn't one.) Things are not always what they seem.

The bipolar disorder is somewhat analogous with diabetes. Diabetes is not considered a psychological disorder, yet, if you catch someone who is having low blood sugar, they can be mean as hell and possibly diagnosable with a personality disorder for that moment. Diabetics may also act intoxicated, but do not necessarily have a substance abuse problem.

A person could be perfectly psychologically fit and if they have the bipolar genes, they are prone to have depressive and manic episodes. They are NOT crazy, although they may act that way because the bipolar disorder deprives them of sleep. Any normal human being who is deprived of sleep long enough may become nasty, delusional, and psychotic, eventually (and temporarily).

Any diagnosis is an art, not a science. It doesn't matter how confident the doctor acts, she/he is just making a professional guess. If he/she is good, she/he will be right most of the time. He/she certainly has more training and education than the average bear, so you should listen to what is said (especially if you are paying for it).

Most people do not like to take medication. The diabetic will take his insulin religiously after having a seizure or blacking out, but then, he usually gets to the point where he says to himself, "You know, I feel pretty good. Maybe the doctors made a mistake. I don't think my pancreas is dead after all." Then he goes off his medication and after a time gloats, "See. I knew it. I am OK. I've been off the meds for a whole week and I feel fine." Then, it might be a week, a month, or a year, and he ends up in the emergency room (ER). You may see him in the ER looking like he has been hit by a train and say, "Hey buddy! What do you think now? Do you think your pancreas is working?" He gives you what he thinks is the proper gesture. Then, after that he may decide that he really does need to take his meds.

I am convinced that "bipolar" is a temperament rather than a disorder. The temperament has its extremes, and then its called the "bipolar disorder", but no one calls it the "bipolar temperament". We have Collies, German Shepherds, Pit Bulls, and Shitzu dogs. All these temperaments have their extremes and all of them react differently to the environment. If you abuse a Collie when it is a puppy, it will probably shy away from people when it grows up. If you abuse a German Shepherd, it will probably bite people when it grows up. If you abuse a Pit Bull, it may kill people when it grows up. If you abuse a Shitzu, it will probably still love people when it grows up... and maybe even become a therapist.

I believe there are a lot of bipolars out there who never need medication, and get along just fine in life. We only see the ones who have unmanageable problems in the psych wards.

Bipolars tend to self-medicate with uppers, downers, and stabilizers. (Cocaine, Alcohol, and Marijuana, for example). When I see this combination at the rehab, I ask, " Do you use substances to <u>feel better</u>, or to get high?"
Most bipolars would answer, "To feel better." or "To feel better AND get high." When a bipolar is "disordered", their thoughts may race (when they are manic) to the point of being overwhelmed and feeling agitated and dispersed. They may use alcohol or heroin to calm themselves down. When they are depressed, they may use cocaine, meth, or some other "upper" to get them out of their depression and help them focus. 60% of bipolars self-medicate. They usually use marijuana as a mood stabilizer, in either case. The problem with self-medication is that it leads to addiction.

Mania operates on dopamine. You can see a similar effect if you give a normal person a bunch of amphetamines. Their eyes look funny, and they are usually talkative, high, and don't sleep much. They will tell you excitedly about all the things they are going to do in life, and have these great ideas about things. It feels good. That's why it is very difficult to treat someone who is elatedly manic. Its like saying, "Hey buddy, you are just toooo happy. We are going to give you some medication that will bring you down to normal again. How'd ya like that!? Hmmm?"
NO WAY!!!

This type of mania might be nice, except that there is a loss of sleep. Anyone who loses sleep significantly for more than a couple days is going to get delusional and maybe psychotic. They usually get paranoid (delusional), angry (due to sleep deprivation), and psychotic if they continue with no sleep. Most of them burn out and go into a depressed state where they may sleep 12 hours a day and feel empty and void. They may have suicidal thoughts. In the manic state of mind, their conscience is not very operational, and they may do things that they regret later (unprotected sex, gambling their savings away, ruining their relationships and friendships, etc). In the depressed mode, they admonish themselves for what they have done, or try to justify what they have done.

Why do they do these things? Don't they have any control? Let me try to explain. The last part of your brain to develop is your pre-frontal lobe area. It should be there about the age of 12, although some people don't even know they have it because they don't use it. The pre-frontal lobe area is that area that is believed to hold the ability to see the big picture of things. It provides you with the IMAGINATION to discern and even be aware what consequences will occur for the action you are taking NOW. People with Attention Deficit Hyperactivity Disorder (ADHD) do not use this function or do not use it much. If you are below the age of 12, you probably don't have it yet. That explains why some people "outgrow" their ADHD. The pre-frontal lobe is also believed to contain the conscience. So when a person is manic ... and their thoughts are racing ... they are preoccupied

COGNITIVELY ... and CONSUMED cognitively to the point where they have no time to FEEL or to be able to imagine how others feel. Cognitively they may be sharp with details, but they are not in touch with their feelings or other's feelings or the consequences of their actions in the present moment. Everything is perceived with logic, which can sometimes be cruel and cold and is very finite (limited).

This is important to understand. So, then you say, "Didn't you know that smoking marijuana could get you expelled from school?"
Their answer is "Yes". They are not stupid, and they COGNITIVELY knew that, but they were not able to IMAGINE it or FEEL it or be CONSCIONABLE about it. In other words, it may not be REAL to them, just some far off intellectual stuff. Those parts of themselves were not working at the time. So they were able to FUNCTION and THINK and may even had brilliant ideas, but their judgment was way off and they had no AWARENESS (just a unattached intellectual understanding) for the consequences or how their actions were going to affect others or even themselves. The general consensus is that the conscience lies in the prefrontal lobes. Mania closes the doors to the prefrontal lobe executive functions (conscience, awareness of consequences, ability to see the big picture, ability to prioritize ... organizational ability).

Example: My mother was normally a very bright woman with a lot of common sense. She could see the bigger picture. But sometimes she would LOSE CONTEXT. My brother called it either "happy crazy" or "bad crazy". When my mother was "happy crazy", she was elated. Everything looked brighter. I remember once when I was 16, I was driving my mother to the electric company in our Volkswagen beetle. The reason we were driving to the electric company is that my mother had to show up with $20 cash or the electric would be shut off. Suddenly as we were driving, she says, "Oh look Jay. A yard sale. Pull over." She jumps out of the car and goes right over to a couch. She says, "Jay, don't you think this is a beautiful color?" I said, "Yes Mom, that's nice." "Oh!", she says, "Look at that! It's only $20! I'm buying this couch!"

Of course, I am worried that she is going to spend the $20 for the electric and we will be without lights. But my mother would lose the bigger picture and not see the consequences until our house was dark. So, I had to try to give her the bigger picture in a tactful way. So, I said, "Mom." "WHAT!", she said (sensing I was going to rain on her parade). "Mom, what are you going to do with the couch at home?" "Oh", she said, "Nothing. I like that couch. It matches the furniture." I reminded her that our living room was not big enough for two couches. She said, "Oh yeah. That's right." Then I asked her how we were going to get the new couch home on top of our Volkswagen Beetle. "Oh yeah", she realized. Then she said, "But it sure is a pretty couch, isn't it." "Yes, Mom. It's a pretty couch."

We drove off to the electric company, then, to pay the electric. Normally, my mother would see the bigger picture, but not when she was manic.

Almost always, you will find (upon investigation) that there is usually someone in their biological family who was bipolar in a previous generation (possibly undiagnosed). It could have been grandpa who was known to do crazy things and drank a lot. It could have been grandma who committed suicide. If the person was adopted, the genetics may have been passed down by one of their biological parents, whose life was unmanageable at the time of pregnancy, having to give the baby up.

The bipolar disorder sometimes appears at the onset of adolescence. However, I have noticed that babies who carry the gene can have an earlier onset if their mother used substances while they were in the womb. There is no research that I know of about this, but in doing speaking engagements across the country for mental health professionals, I have gotten a lot of consensus about this. Manic behavior in children can get misdiagnosed as Attention Deficit Hyperactivity Disorder. If they are put on ritalin, then, they really get crazy. Psychostimulants (ritalin, adderol, cocaine, meth, etc.) can cause psychotic homicidal behavior in someone who is manic. Caffeine is a no-no for bipolars. Most bipolar children are rapid cyclers. The psycho-stimulant may appear to help them focus until the child cycles to mania. Then the child can become suicidal or homicidal. It can be very dangerous.

Some manic behavior is not hereditary, but is merely due to the effects of drugs on the brain chemistry (Eg: Someone who was "Robotripping" with Robitussen). It <u>looks</u> like the person has a bipolar disorder, but does not re-occur if the person stops using substances. Of course, most bipolars have the wishful thinking that this is what must have happened to them, and they are the exception, so they don't really need to take a mood stabilizer the rest of their lives. Right! Fat chance!

When I interview an adolescent girl who has her hair died pink, has had sex with six guys in the past month, and who admits to using cocaine, alcohol, and marijuana, I suspect bipolar problems. It is important to sit down with this person and explain the bipolar disorder. I usually let them read the symptoms right out of the DSM IV (The Psychiatric Bible), and let them decide for themselves if they are bipolar. Many are very relieved to find that they have a chemical problem, rather than think that they are inherently evil or a bad seed. It gives them a new lease on life, and hope for the future.

For some bipolars, their first diagnosis can be an epiphany. They will say, "You mean, I wasn't responsible for all the nasty things I said to people, and my temper tantrums? My moods were actually significantly more intense than other people? My sex drive was much higher than others? You mean, I am not a bad person? I'm not just a bad seed?"

The epiphany gives them absolution, and then I say, "That's right. But now that you know this, and you know there is medication for it ... you ARE responsible for it from now on."

If you have never been manic, then you wouldn't know what it is like. Some people get an unbelievable sex drive when they are manic. Remember when you were an adolescent and you had a hard time resisting sexual activity? Well, times that by ten. See what I mean ?

Sleep deprivation is usually a secondary problem to the bipolar disorder, yet it is a problem which causes delusions, paranoia, anger, and sometimes psychosis. LACK OF SLEEP probably accounts for the most significant problems with the bipolar disorder. It is most important for someone who tends to be bipolar to get the proper sleep. A reduction in sleep or a time zone change (interruption in circadian rhythm) can propel a person into a manic episode (<u>Time Magazine</u>, August 19, 2002). Bipolars should never work swing shifts or midnight shifts. Another thing that affects bipolar kids is family disruptions (same Time article).

THE PSYCHIATRIC "BIBLE"

The DSM IV is the psychiatric "bible" for professionals (The American Psychiatric Association's Diagnostic and Statistical Manual of Mental Disorders). However it was never meant to be a bible. It is a description of various symptoms and the categorization of these groups of symptoms. It doesn't necessarily contain "everything". Although it is fairly complete, it doesn't have all the mental health problems described that we will ever run into. The DSM always has been a "work in progress". For example, the description of a bipolar child is not in the DSM. The description in the DSM is for adults, while children exhibit differently. The DSM IV contains the symptoms that doctors look for to diagnose the bipolar disorder. It's only fair that I give you this adapted information as well as my own personal experience.

In order to be diagnosed bipolar, a person must have at least one manic or hypomanic episode. This episode must be 4 to 7 days of being abnormally "high" or angry-manic. Three of the next seven symptoms must be present consistently:
- big ego and think they are the greatest
- not sleeping much and not needing sleep
- talkative beyond their normal talkativeness
- racing thoughts
- easily distracted
- hyper-focused or goal oriented
- high risk behavior (promiscuity, unprotected sex, over-spending, drug abuse, etc.)

These symptoms must be consistent, last four days or more, and be abnormal for that individual.

If the person becomes so manic that they have to be admitted to a hospital, the "four days or more" is not needed to diagnose it. I would also add "mood swings" as indicative of the bipolar disorder. The requirement for diagnosis is mania for 4 to 7 days, but you can surely ruin your life in one afternoon of mania.

A child doesn't present like an adult. Depression in a child is, many times, indicated by irritability or "boredom". Most bipolar kids are rapid-cyclers (up and down) while most adults show more definitive periods of depression and mania (angry or euphoric).

In extreme cases where the person has become psychotic, they are medicated with an anti-depressant, mild anti-psychotic drug, and a mood stabilizer. An anti-depressant is used because a person who becomes manic "burns up" their serotonin (an anti-depressant chemical) during the manic phase and a depression almost always follows. After an episode, they could have up to 40% less serotonin in the brain. The lack of serotonin is associated with depression and hostility. They are psychotic or delusional from lack of sleep and need an anti-psychotic to think straight and help them to sleep. They need a mood stabilizer to keep them from getting manic again. Of course, it is possible to have such a sudden dopamine imbalance, that one becomes psychotic quickly, but in most cases it is from lack of sleep.

After a time, the anti-psychotic drug is taken away. The anti-depressant is usually taken away after a couple of months, and the mood stabilizer stays. The mood stabilizer to a bipolar is like insulin is to a diabetic. It fosters a balance. The doctor adjusts the mood stabilizer as time goes on.

Antipsychotics are used in place of (or in addition to) mood stabilizers to maintain someone who is bipolar. A concern I have, is that some bipolars say they feel "anxiety". This "anxiety" is most likely physical agitation, not anxiety. The Antipsychotics may not do as well as the mood stabilizers to curb the physical agitation. This is very important since the suicide rate for bipolars who feel "anxiety" is much higher than bipolars who do not. It is 30 times higher than the general population for anxiety bipolars and 7 times higher for the other bipolars. The suicide rate in general for bipolars is almost 20%. That is a very high death rate. If suicide occurs, it is usually within the first two years of the onset of diagnosable symptoms.

Some bipolars have episodes of mania, whereas others will become manic immediately upon stopping their medication. It's very tempting to some of them to stop taking their medication so they can get high. They end up being addicted to their own brain chemicals. They have fun while it lasts, but depression is right around the next corner. Other bipolars have seasonal episodes. They may only get manic during April and May, or during the winter. In any case, the psychiatrist usually puts them on medication for the whole year. The danger with stopping and starting medication is that the judgement of the patient becomes too impaired to be compliant with his/her medication. This is due to the inability to see the big picture or the consequences as shown in the last chapter (prefrontal lobe capability) and described in a following chapter; "Reasonable Explanations". If she/he gets manic, she/he is very likely to have a full blown episode which may ruin her/his life with the manic behavior and the mania "burn out".

The anti-depressants used are usually the serotonin medications (SSRI's). I sometimes call them "serotonin vitamins", because they are not like the old generation drugs that were blockers or anesthesizers so that a person was so sedated they didn't even know they were depressed. Twenty years ago, I was visiting a bipolar friend in the psychiatric ward who was on some of those old drugs, and I said, "These anti-depressants really wipe you out, huh?"
He sat there all lethargic in his hospital nightie with food spilled on it with his wispy uncombed hair and said, "Yeah, the meds make me stupid, but I am getting so degraded now, that I am starting to like it." For all he had been through, his sense of humor was still in tact.

The anti-psychotics used today are usually Respirdal, or Zyprexa, which are the newer milder anti-psychotics and do not have the same major mental side effects as the old drugs such as thorazine causing the "thorazine shuffle" which you may have seen in the old psychiatric wards like in the movie "One Flew Over the Cuckoo's Nest". The newest one as of this writing is Abilify (FDA approved June, 2003) which seems to have good results for some and very little side effects, but some people have found it ineffective or gotten sick from it too (consensus of seminar attendees who have seen it used). The mood stabilizers are usually Lithium (which has been around for a long time and is still effective), Depakote, Tegretol, or Neurontin. The newest FDA approved mood stabilizer as of this writing is Lamictal (FDA Nov. 2002) which seems to work for some rapid cyclers that no other medication has worked for. The major side effect with Lamictal is a skin rash that can be deadly. The rash can look like measles or as bad as hamburger. If you see a rash after taking Lamictal, call the doctor ... NOW. Sometimes this rash can be avoided by slowly introducing Lamictal. For most adults there is no rash problem, but for children, it is more likely. Topamax is one of the few mood stabilizers with the side effect of weight loss. It was recently approved by the FDA for weight loss programs (Nov. 2003?) whether you were bipolar or not. There is some uncertainty as to how well Topamax affects mood stabilization for some. One psychiatrist used Gabitril with Topamax for mood stabilization and weight loss for her overweight bipolar clients. Most of the meds are associated with weight gain, especially Lithium and Zyprexa, although these are very effective for emotional stabilization. Some of these are extracts. Tegretol is a synthetic drug. These drugs need to be checked for blood levels to make sure they are not too high and to make sure the body absorbs a therapeutic level. Lithium is a salt, so it has to be monitored like any salt. Depakote is valproic acid (as citrus is an acid) and must be monitored for that reason. Tegretol sometimes affects the liver and liver enzymes must be checked. If a patient has a damaged liver, Tegretol is contraindicated (shouldn't be used). Trileptal is made from Tegretol and is a better Tegretol, albeit more expensive. The consensus is that it has very few side effects. As I travel across the country, it is the one medication that seems to stand out above all other newer medications. Neurontin is newer in its use as a mood stabilizer and has had success. It usually has very few side effects and is safe. A general consensus says that it leaves some patients a little bit manic (which they like), but helps them with their sleep. Recent research shows that it can also treat depression. However, there is some question as to how effective it is in the long run for mood stabilization. The minimum dose for Neurontin, Lithium, and Depakote is usually 300 mg. three times a day. Neurontin can go to 900 mg. three times a day. Lithium can go to 2400 mg. a day and Depakote to 1500 mg. a day. Tegretol can go from 600 to 1600 mg. a day. The dosage of these drugs varies according to the weight of a person, serum blood level checks, and the tolerance as perceived by the doctor. In extreme cases, lithium may be used with another mood stabilizer since it seems to enhance the effectiveness of some other drugs. Fluid intake should be monitored by someone taking Lithium. Some renal failure has been known to develop in 20 or 30 years with lithium. You may have to choose between suicide at 25 or 30% renal failure at 55.

Since Lithium is a salt, there is some weight gain. Depakote is also associated with weight gain for some people and some people find a little more hair in the drain after a shower. No, it doesn't mean you will go bald. Neurontin seems to work well, at first, for most people, but it seems to lose its effectiveness for some and has to be increased in dosage. Topamax is a newer recommendation as of this writing, since it has the side effect of weight loss and has been used for seizure disorders in children for years. As of this writing, I have personally seen it used with several people. One was a strong bipolar and it allowed her to go into a manic state. One was a mild bipolar and it seemed to work at times during the day, but manic symptoms could still be seen including some sleep loss and angry-manic behavior. One was a child, who also experienced sporadic daily improvement, but some manic behavior (albeit <u>less</u> manic). It seems to take several months to stabilize and during those several months the patient may be at risk. There is a website for the Mayo Clinic where there is a psychiatrist who advocates for Topamax.

This book is by no means a scientific study, just phenomenological observations of many professionals (psychiatric nurses, therapists, psychologists, doctors who attend my seminars) along with a warning to be careful with your expectations of ANY medication. Different medications work for different people. If someone is bipolar and taking a "serotonin vitamin" (SSRI's like Prozac, Paxil, Effexor, Luvox), Topamax may prevent a manic episode ... and weight gain. One of the side effects of the SSRI's is possible mania if the person has the bipolar genes and is not given a mood stabilizer. Luvox has the worst reputation for this, but Zoloft is less likely to foster a manic episode, according to consensus. I personally believe there are a lot of different types of bipolar out there. When these types are discerned better, there will be a better possibility of getting the right medication the first time.

A good way of classifying might be "Bipolar with Agitation (anxiety)" (calling for a mood stabilizer) and "Bipolar without Agitation (without anxiety)" calling for either a mood stabilizer or anti-psychotic. Another way of classifying might be to identify the temperament of a person. It seems that some medications work better on certain temperaments. Temperament is not concrete or finite, but it can help to ball-park someone to match the medication. So far, no one has come up with a system like this.

There are two more mood stabilizers that have come to my attention from doing seminars across the country. One is Geodon, which has been reported to be successful in non-violent people. There was one prison that stopped using it because they thought it provoked violence in their patients. Don't forget, there ARE some violent people in jail, bipolar or not. The other drug which I have heard "miracle" stories about is Lamictal. One story is from a psychologist whose brother was bipolar and had been living on the streets for ten years. He was a rapid cycler and no medication seemed to help him until Lamictal. Lamictal stabilized him and he was able to work, and in fact, became a manager. His employer is very happy with him. He did have the side effect of his face feeling rashy, but no rash appeared. It was much better than the side effect of being homeless for ten years.

So there you have many of the standard phenomenological limits and boundaries of bipolar disorder treatment by medication, for now. It is liable to get better with new medication discoveries. The meds are better than ever, but keep in mind the plight of the person with the bipolar disorder. Some of these drugs cause frequent urination, weight gain, and sexual side effects. Besides that, the euphoric mania may be addictive and enticing. Some people take meds and feel <u>right</u>. Others don't feel right, but take them just to make their lives more manageable. It is not very empathetic to say, "If they just took their meds, they would be OK." If you think it's that simple, you may need a shot of Thorazine in the butt and see if <u>you</u> feel OK after that.

BIPOLAR STORIES

Some bipolars have a severe disorder, others moderate, and others mild. These stories are about unidentifiable people and serve to clarify, in human experience, what the bipolar disorder can be like.

The Lord

A man came to prison and I was asked to interview him. The person who asked me to talk to him snickered and raised his eyebrow, so I knew something was up. I went down to the intake cell block and found a young male. Evidently, he had been picked up on cocaine possession charges and hadn't slept in weeks. The first question I asked was, "What is your name?"

He responded, "I am the Lord."

I looked at him to see if he was kidding. He wasn't. I knew it was going to a rough day, then. And, in case you ever wondered ... the Lord has blue eyes and long blonde hair.

At this point I knew he was psychotic or delusional (unless he really was the Lord, of course), but I didn't know if he was schizophrenic or had cocaine-induced psychosis. It didn't matter since the treatment was the same. In jail he was going to get Haldol which is an inexpensive, but effective anti-psychotic. He agreed to take any medication we wanted to give him and seemed glad to do it. The Haldol knocked him out for a couple days, and in the meantime I did some research. I found out that his drugs of choice were cocaine, alcohol and marijuana. He had been in the streets talking to everyone he could, about whatever he could (talkative and pressure to keep talking). He had spent all of his money on prostitutes and frequented them several times a day. (Hypersexuality). He hadn't slept much even before the cocaine and was starting to seem depressed at the point he started using it. He was normally a nice quiet kid who smoked marijuana all the time. He had held a steady job and loved to work.

After he slept for a couple days, I brought him into my office and showed him the manic symptoms in the DSM IV. He acknowledged them as his own. He told me that he had an Uncle Harry that was like that and eventually committed suicide. We put him on Depakote and he slept a lot after that. After a couple days, he told me that he didn't want to take the Depakote because it made him sleep too much. I explained to him that the Depakote was NOT making him sleep. It was just getting his body to recognize that he did, in reality, need sleep. After a month, he was stabilized on the Depakote and getting normal sleep with normal wake time.

He laughed about being the Lord.

The day after "the Lord" left, Napoleon came to the jail. Napoleon had been up for two weeks doing cocaine. I diagnosed him quicker than the Lord.

The Bank Robber

I was asked to testify for a man who had robbed six banks in another state. This man had raised a family. He was in his late forties and had no criminal record. He had recently separated from his wife after 23 years of marriage. She was seeing another man. He had been a heavy drinker and had bouts of rage, but had never physically abused his family. He had gotten into a couple bar room skirmishes, but nothing serious. He was an executive for a construction company and had raised four children.

All six banks wanted him to do five years each. That was a total of 30 years for a first offense. When he robbed the banks, he had done so politely, thanking the tellers for filling his paper bag with money and apologizing for himself. He would have gotten away with it, except he parked in front of the police barracks to rob the last bank. His license plate had been dangling off the back of his car, so when he came out of the bank with the paper bag full of money, there was an officer looking at his plate. The officer told him he needed to affix his plate better, so he threw the bag of money in the back seat and the officer helped him tighten his license plate. He drove off, thanking the officer. When the officer heard about the bank robbery, he saw the bank video and was surprised to see it was the guy he helped with the license plate, but remembered the license plate number and that's how they caught him.

The man was sure his wife would come back to him if he had enough money, so he bet all his money at the races and kept robbing banks to bet on the races. He was sure he would win with his "system" and then he would give all the money back and recover his fortune.

He was diagnosed bipolar in prison and was

getting a mood stabilizer and anti-depressant. His relatives and friends visited him in jail and said he was back to normal.

There were two problems with his case. One problem was that each bank wanted him to do five years, and the other was that he pre-meditated the robberies and therefore (the argument was) that he was not insane at the time of the robberies because they were not spontaneous reactions.

Yes, he pre-meditated the robberies, but they were pre-meditated by someone who was MANIC. The banks relented the five years each, but then each county wanted five years. He had robbed banks in four different counties. Finally, after the judge understood the bipolar disorder more clearly, he adjudicated that he could do the time for all six banks and four counties in one five year sentence. It was the right thing to do. The man was not a criminal. He was bipolar.

There are many bipolars in jail who do not belong there. They can be treated with medication and the medication can easily be checked in their blood levels. They are examples of how mania can ruin someone's life. Of course, there are bipolars who are bipolar and nurture a criminal intent. They should not be released. But the undiagnosed or unmedicated bipolars who have had a manic episode should be considered for work release as long as they agree to take medication and are checked regularly for therapeutic blood levels. I have submitted a proposal to the Governor of Pennsylvania and the Governor of Hawaii for such a program.

I believe people should take responsibility for

what they do, or they never get better (even if it's not their fault). But as a taxpayer, and knowing what I know ... a man or woman like this can take better responsibility by working to pay back the money, not by sitting in jail. Someone who is bipolar may do something crazy in a manic-moment and then <u>we</u> have to pay to incarcerate her/him, and we have to support his/her children on welfare while confined in prison. Well, it doesn't make sense to me unless it was a personal injury crime, in which case the victim should have a say.

Sarah

Sarah was a pretty 14 year old girl who lived in a small town. Her father had been diagnosed as bipolar and died at the age of 35 from AIDS. Prior to being diagnosed, he was hypersexual (sexually driven) and abused drugs including intravenous drugs. Lithium was the only mood stabilizer that worked for him. After he was on Lithium, he was able to control his sexuality and his mania. By then, it was too late, since he was already HIV positive.

Mania can sometimes bring on hypersexuality. The best way to explain it is to compare it to thirst. The person can have ten times the sexual drive a normal person has. It is as if you were without water and were desperately thirsty. After a while, you would do anything for water.

This little fourteen year old sneaked out of the house one night in a manic state and met the neighbor kids at an abandoned house. There were eight adolescent boys and her girlfriend. That night she had 25 shots of liquor in her 90 pound body.

She ended up having sex with all eight boys voluntarily and instigated on her own. She continued in her mania for a couple more days and then crashed into a depression. After she realized that she had ruined her reputation, she made a genuine attempt to commit suicide. She was in a psychiatric hospital several times after that and was given various mood stabilizers. She kept telling the doctors that she needed lithium. After trying everything else, she was finally given lithium and it stabilized her mood.

Many times, the same drugs work for the same family.

Her sexual behavior was NOT a case of morality, but a case of mania. That doesn't mean that someone uses the bipolar disorder for an excuse and gets off, but bipolar disorders are real and the disorder really does cause people to do things they would never do otherwise. Now that she knows this, she knows that she needs to take her medication so it doesn't happen again.

Billy the Kid

There was a kid in prison who was 18 years old. He was in for stealing money with MAC machine cards that he made up himself. He was a very bright kid, and I liked him. He had robbed a bank that had charged me extra at a closing and I secretly was glad he had ripped them off, since they seem to be able to rip people off "legally". Billy (not his real name) was a computer whiz. He had gotten a computer job on work release and drove his car everyday from the prison to work. One day he drove out of the prison driveway and didn't come back.

He did not show up for work that day. After two weeks, he turned himself back in to the warden. He was charged with escape and more time was added to his sentence. He was put in the "hole" for 30 days. It was my job to check the psychological well-being of inmates in the disciplinary block (the "hole"). When I talked to him, I asked him what happened. He said he didn't know. He said he just drove out of the driveway and got this "feeling" and decided he didn't need to go back. For two weeks he earned his keep playing pool and sleeping at different women's homes. He was very promiscuous, drank a lot, and didn't sleep much. He said he came to his senses two weeks later, and turned himself in. He didn't know why he left and couldn't believe he did it.

In checking with his mother, I found out that his grandfather had been in and out of the state hospital many times and eventually committed suicide. It was a family secret and they didn't talk about it. She also said that Billy had been a great kid up until his adolescence. He was a straight "A" student and well behaved. Then, when his adolescence started, he began staying up until all hours of the night and hanging out with a bad element. He started drinking every night with his friends and she couldn't control him.

After more evidence, I diagnosed him as bipolar. When he talked with me about the symptoms of mania, he was amazed to see that I "knew him so well". Good luck Billy, wherever you are.

One Time Forgiveness

Sometimes there are two or more problems operating within a person. There was a seventeen year old girl who came to prison. Evidently, she had resisted arrest and the police had to force her into the back of the police car. When she was back there she kicked the window out with her shoes (A very difficult feat). When I interviewed her in jail, she seemed like a very sweet girl. She had been going to college and getting all A's. She said she couldn't remember everything about the night she was arrested (but, of course, that's what a lot of criminals say). The police tested her for all kinds of drugs because they were sure she was high on something. The tests were negative and it was a general consensus that she got away with a drug charge. However, she had plenty of other charges that she could be incarcerated for such as, resisting arrest, speeding, and destroying government property.

After interviewing her, I realized she was having a manic episode the day she was arrested and was just speeding down the highway with the radio blasting. The police pulled her over and she was manic-angry with grandiosity, arrogance, and sense of entitlement (typical manic symptoms). She was acting like she was "on" something so the police felt led to investigate. They did not know that her behavior was totally out of character for her. It was similar to pulling over a diabetic that was acting intoxicated.

Her grandmother had been manic-depressive, and was known for running off and doing crazy things. This girl was having these manic episodes (not knowing what they were) and was doing things she would not ordinarily do. The only part that had me puzzled was her strong reaction to being put into the police car. Obviously her adrenaline was running. Adrenaline can give a human being two or three times their normal strength and she would have had to be on adrenaline (or PCP) to kick that window out. I asked her about that and she said she thought the police were trying to rape her. She also added that she knew they weren't really, but couldn't help her reaction.

In talking to her mother, the answer came to light. She had been raped by three men when she was thirteen, and yes they forced her into the back seat of a car to do it. They all went to jail, but it left her traumatized.

So, there were two things operating inside of her; the trauma, and the mania.

I wrote a letter to the judge explaining the above. I added something that I don't usually add. I gave my opinion of justice. (Judges don't usually like that from psychologists, or anyone else, for that matter. That's their job!). I couldn't help it. I suggested that if there was ever any such thing as a "one time forgiveness", that she should have it. There was at least one hard-ass jail shrink who had tears in his eyes when the judge dropped the charges.

I heard she is graduating from college soon on the Dean's list. She is happily married and she takes her Depakote religiously.

The Business Addict

Some time ago, there was a man who was admitted to the Caron Foundation for a cocaine, alcohol, and marijuana addiction. He was going nowhere and his life was a mess. He was beating up his girlfriend. He was fired from his job.

He managed to kick his drug problems and never touched it again. He was a good worker and obsessed with doing a good job. He started a business and ten years later he had several employees. He was making a lot of money.

He was still beating up his girlfriend. It usually happened in January and February. She was not the type to take it and was breaking up with him. He was devastated. In a counseling session with him, she said that all year long he was a beautiful human being. It was just January and February that he got physically aggressive. He came in for counseling and ended up back with his girlfriend. He wanted to marry her, but she was afraid he would become abusive. The next January, he started showing changes in counseling. His attitude changed. He wasn't sleeping at night and became paranoid about his workers ripping him off. He would get in their faces and then regret it after. Like many bipolars, he was generally very personable, but would get annoyed with people depending on his mood. Sometimes he would get annoyed with people in general. He would notice something he did not like about someone (like a wart on their nose), and was smart enough to know that it was not OK to be upset at something like that, so he would find another reason to attack them. He had an incident where he beat up a drunk driver. He started making physical gestures at his girlfriend and was argumentative with her. He was talkative during the sessions and would dominate the session. Sometimes he would say things that were even detrimental to himself. His brain seemed connected to his tongue without the prefrontal lobe filtering system engaged. Mania can be like a truth serum.

He reluctantly agreed to take Lithium. So, during January and February he slept twelve hours a night. He was laid back at work and his workers were relieved. His girlfriend was relieved. He hated it. He said it made him too slow. He complained that it interfered with his creativity and he wasn't as sharp. (Actually, it just brought his mental speed to normal, like the rest of us mortals). He stopped taking it in March and started getting his usual six hours sleep.

He is now a very successful businessman and he is married to this girlfriend. He has not hit her in five years. However, he has agreed that when she tells him to take his lithium, he will take it. Around January and February every year, he ends up taking his medication. He hates it. Everyone else loves it. For two months he eases up on everyone and sleeps twelve hours a day. For the other ten months, he is hypomanic. He thinks faster than other people. He is a shrewd businessman. He is charming, generous, funny, and has no qualms about getting in your face if you are inappropriate.

In other words, he manages the disorder well.

Bipolars are usually hard workers. They liven the place up and keep people on their toes. There are many successful bipolars. They get obsessed with their goals and do not give up. He is an example of a mild to moderate bipolar who has his life in order. He depends on trusted people to tell him when he is getting out of hand and then submits to them (difficult to do when manic). Between his great abilities, the people who he is connected to, and his wealth, I would say his life is not just manageable, but excellent.

Bipolar Kids

There are not enough good child psychiatrists in many parts of the country. There is some controversy about medicating children to begin with, so professionals are reluctant to do so. In my experience with children, I found that six out of a hundred children in the Pennsylvania Wraparound Program, who came to my office were misdiagnosed with Attention Deficit Hyperactivity Disorder (ADHD), when they should have been diagnosed as bipolar-manic. We have excellent professionals here, so I would assume there is about 6% misdiagnoses in other parts of the country as well. The consensus as I travel around the country is that there are 6 to 10% of the kids being misdiagnosed for ADHD when they are actually bipolar. This seems to be improving as we learn to discern and the therapists learn more about what to expect from medication.

A good bipolar therapist would have some knowledge as to whether a certain behavior was coming from:
1. The bipolar disorder,
2. The medication, or
3. A possible behavioral/psychological problem.

Kids do not usually act depressed. They act bored or angry, instead. Young children who are bipolar usually act manic (elated, angry-manic, violent). 93% of bipolar children appear to have every symptom of ADHD, but they are manic. People in the schools are taught to recognize the symptoms of ADHD, but not mania. With mania, the child usually does not sleep the normal amount of hours for his age. (For example: A six year old can't sleep until midnight, then wakes up at six AM). They also are distracted, NOT because they have ADHD, but because they have racing thoughts. They are hostile and angry because these are the usual symptoms of anyone who doesn't get enough sleep. They have mood swings. BUT, if you distract a child who is manic from something he really wants, he will GO BACK to that thing. Someone who has ADHD usually, will not go back.

Out of 150 children I saw in the Wraparound program, I re-diagnosed 9 of them with the bipolar disorder. These children had all been on Ritalin, which is a psychostimulant. Psychiatrists know that a psychostimulant is contraindicated in someone who is manic. It can make them homicidal, and that is exactly what it did to three of these children. These children were considered severe behavioral problems. Some would have periods of unconscionable behavior followed by periods of remorse. The three who became homicidal were admitted to an inpatient children's unit where they were switched to Adderol (still a psychostimulant) and given an anti-psychotic for sleep. When they were released, the homicidal behavior stopped, but the manic behavior persisted, of course. Eight of these children were switched to Neurontin and one older child was given Depakote. The change was considered miraculous by some teachers and parents. Most of these kids were considered "bullies" and did poorly academically. After the switch in medication, 7 became A students. Two were mixed A's & B's. They stopped bullying the other children. The mood swings greatly improved. They were able to pay attention without the racing thoughts, and improve their behavior. It really was close to miraculous. One boy, who was 13, ended up taking Depakote because the Neurontin was not effective enough for him.

Their behavior changed to the point where most of them were considered charming, intelligent, well-behaved children. Amazing, huh!?

Most of the children I saw were probably not going to see a psychiatrist. It was too difficult to get authorization, or time consuming, or not covered in the medical plan. However, there are many family physicians that are willing to prescribe Neurontin or Topamax because these drugs have been used on children before for seizure disorders. Neurontin is used for seizures and headaches. Doctor's don't mind using 200 mg of Neurontin at bedtime for a child. It is non-toxic and the minimum dose for an adult is 300mg, three times a day. The physician can go to CABF.ORG or the Mayo clinic website and get information about bipolar symptoms and the recommended drugs. If 200 mg. of Neurontin shows a good improvement, but not quite enough, then another 200 mg. in the morning is usually added. The child may seem tired for a couple of weeks, but that is probably because they need to catch up on their sleep. After a couple weeks the child should be sleeping regularly.

Some other pointers:

- Bipolar kids have a grandiosity not usually seen in ADHD kids

- An ADHD kid will rage for 12 to 20 minutes until the adrenaline is gone. A bipolar kid will rage on for a much longer time.

- An ADHD kid may have a bad dream about someone chasing him with a knife, and wake up just before he gets stabbed. The bipolar kid may dream right through the stabbing with all the blood and guts.

- A child who is manic is thinking thinking thinking. I have seen intensive cognitive thought trigger manic episodes in some children and in college students.

- A bipolar child may be sexually oriented. This may lead to the perception that the child is eroticized and therefore has been sexually abused. Actually, only 1% of bipolar children have been sexually abused (Popolos, 2002).

BALANCING

There are two major psychological goals which should be most important to someone who is bipolar:

1. Most importantly, getting enough sleep and having a structured sleep cycle is the thing that counts the most for preventing episodes and mood swings. Never work third shift. Never work swing shifts. Be very careful when traveling in different time zones, because a circadian rhythm change can seriously affect sleep.
2. Make sure life is structured. That seems to be

the second most important item for adult bipolars to balance their lives. Bipolars are known for thinking out of the box, but they have to have a box to think out of. A structured life is that box. For a bipolar child, a structured life is just as important as the sleep factor. Having a routine is necessary.

Maintaining a balanced life is the most difficult task for the bipolar. Some have mood swings that are very high and very low. Some have periods of intense mania and intense depression. For others ("soft" bipolars), the mood swings are tolerable and they can handle them psychologically. Their mania and low periods are tolerable and they do not have suicidal ideation.

Some require medication to function, and there are some excellent medications now for the bipolar disorder. Soft bipolars do not absolutely require medication, but their friends and relatives wish that they would take some, anyway. It may help a lot in their relationships, impulsiveness, and ability to see the bigger picture. I am sure there are some people with this temperament who are perfectly fine without medication and have no "technical difficulties" with their mind or body despite the "big engine" they have. For a mild bipolar disorder, why not have a little Neurontin available when the sleep gets deprived? Its non-addictive, and I believe that some people could be trusted in their own judgement to take it as needed. Perhaps the doctor would be willing to prescribe a couple Seroquel tablets for sleep emergencies. After a couple nights of not getting sleep, a person who is bipolar is either on the brink of a manic episode, or already in an episode. If there are too many sleep emergencies, it may be time to adjust the medication.

It is very helpful for a bipolar (or anyone) to have a purpose in life. If you don't have a purpose, maybe your purpose could be to <u>find out</u> what your purpose is. If there is something to focus on, it cuts down on the "spinning". On a good day, you may be able to accomplish a couple days work. Then there are those bad days that you may not be able to accomplish anything. Besides the use of medication, which can help, there is the old school of thought of developing discipline and organization. In these times the old schools tend to be forgotten in pursuit of the seemingly easier prospect of medication. You have to know when to hold 'em and when to fold 'em. That's the big trick, and part of that big trick is being able to take direction and advice from a trusted friend, relative, or doctor. Besides help with medication, it may be valuable to have a friend or relative that encourages following through with projects. Otherwise your life may get cluttered with unfinished projects. Other people who are bipolar may need help in quitting a project they may be obsessed with if there is no end in sight and if it is making life unmanageable.

Self Medication

As I stated before, bipolars tend to self medicate with an upper (cocaine, meth), a downer (alcohol, heroin, etc.), and a stabilizer (marijuana). If you have ever smoked marijuana, you know its a great mood stabilizer. There's only the one mood, man. The drug they use depends on whether their mind is racing, they feel depressed, or they feel agitated. These drugs carry the side effects of addiction, and they are illegal which carries the consequence of jail time. In addition, they alter the judgement of a person and are hard to regulate (and sometimes hard to obtain). There is the question of purity, quality, toxicity, and overdose.

Psychotropic Medication

If you are going to medicate yourself "anyway", then you may as well get the advice and experience of a professional. The side effects will be less and the risk is much less. It could even cost less than using illegal substances if you have a good HMO!

I find it ironical when I get someone who is using cocaine, marijuana, and alcohol, and the first thing they say to me after I offer them to be evaluated by a psychiatrist is, "Nope. I don't want to take any prescription drugs." I don't like taking drugs either, but after I read an autopsy of someone who used a lot of cocaine with all the brain "lesions" and dead spots, I'll take Depakote or Lithium any day. If I ruined my marriage by having sex and getting a disease from a manic episode ... yeah, give me a mood stabilizer and a serotonin vitamin, man. And if I'm in jail for possession, give me that Neurontin, after all. I mean, I like Billy and all, but I just don't want to be his cell mate.

Biofeedback

There has been some success without drugs. Biofeedback is a method whereby brain waves are measured. We have Alpha, Beta, and Theta brain waves. Bipolars are usually very <u>cognitive</u> (they think, think, think). Because they are so consumed with thought, they don't have time to <u>feel</u> (hence the conscience by the back door). In a biofeedback session, a personal computer is hooked up to a biofeedback machine, which is hooked up to the head by those same things you get hooked up for an electrocardiogram. It measures brain waves and can tell whether you are <u>thinking</u>, and how much you are thinking. It's really amazing, state of the art stuff. Luckily it can't tell <u>what</u> you are thinking or we would all be in trouble. If you exhibit "type A" waves, you get a minus-one. If you exhibit "type B" waves, you get a plus-one. The whole idea is to win the computer game with pluses and teach your mind to think (or should I say <u>not</u> to think so much). Again, <u>balance</u> is the most important factor. These biofeedback machines are also good for Attention Deficit Disorder and claim that 65% of the kids on medication do not need it anymore after training their minds. But keep in mind the bipolar disorder is <u>chemical</u> and <u>hereditary</u>. Psychological interventions will help, but it is a physiological problem.

So, instead of getting overwhelmed with racing thoughts, the bipolar can focus his/her attention of other things until the thoughts are like a radio playing in the background, and you do not have to listen to it. You can turn up the volume anytime you wish, but only if you want to. It becomes a <u>choice</u> instead of being overwhelmed and imprisoned by your thoughts.

These biofeedback places usually give free tours. Take one. It is truly amazing.

Like people with Attention Deficit Disorder, sometimes bipolars have trouble seeing the "big picture" of a situation. They may get nitty-gritty and "anal" about the details <u>without</u> seeing the bigger scope. They end up winning arguments and losing the relationships. A bipolar man may be surprised after winning all the marital arguments only to watch his wife as she walks off into the sunset wishing him "Happy Trails".

Someone who is bipolar should try not to beat up helpful friends and relatives. You might need to borrow their prefrontal lobes when yours aren't working so well.

THERAPISTS

Bipolars know whether the therapist understands them or not. If the therapist can somewhat understand the mentality and behavior and discern the source of it (medication? bipolar? psychological?), the client may not quit so soon. People who are bipolar seem to respond to nurturing more than rationalizations, and insight. The National Institute for Mental Health recommends family involvement and education. NIMH recommends Cognitive Behavioral Therapy specifically for the bipolar disorder. Psychotherapy is useful when a prefrontal lobe is working, but when it isn't, all insight goes out the window, and the bipolar client has to rely on concrete rules and goals ... and it is more helpful if these things are WRITTEN. 9% of the time, mania is euphoric. The other 91% of the time, it is angry/rageful. It has been shown that hostility is most successfully addressed with nurturing (Anger Kills). That has been my personal experience in growing up with a bipolar mother, working at the jail, and the Caron foundation. I have been with thousands of people who are bipolar and manic and never once had anyone commit a violent act upon me. Yet, it has been found that people being admitted to a facility who are manic commit a violent act (spitting, pushing, hitting, stabbing, shooting) 50% of the time. Is that because of those nasty bipolar people out there? Or ... could it be that we know so little about them that we provoke them to be violent? I think the later. You know that bully down the road who beats up your kid? What does that bully need? Nurturing. What is going to work? Nurturing. What is the very thing you don't FEEL like giving that kid? Nurturing. Is it going to work all the time? Not until you get good at it. Also, there are some bipolars who ARE violent besides being bipolar. Nurturing will help, but be prepared to duck.

One of the latest discoveries is that the Omega 3 fatty acids seem to balance out medication. Even if a person is on medication, they have peaks and valleys. Omega 3 is not a substitute for medication, but helps makes the medication more consistent. One psychiatrist recommends 2000 milligrams a day. I understand there is a "burpless" type available now at the health food stores.

BIPOLAR MANIC BRAIN DYSFUNCTION

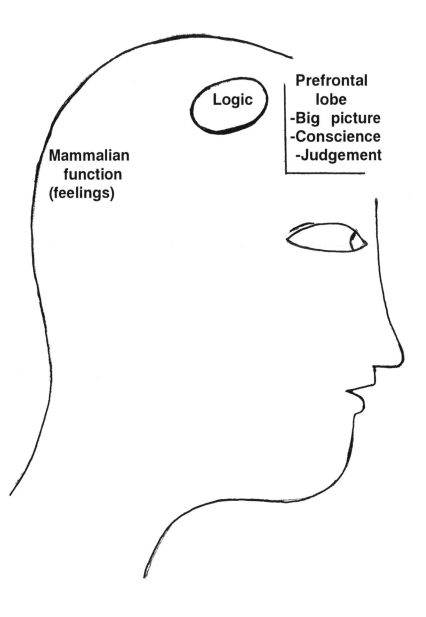

REASONABLE EXPLANATIONS

Intervening
   Note the diagram on the adjacent page ←—.
The Intervention for someone who is manic is:
1. Get them in their prefrontal lobe.
2. Get them in touch with their feelings.
How do you get someone in the prefrontal lobe? By reminding them of the bigger picture and showing concern for them. When they are manic, they do not seem to process new information well, so you need to remind them of a past situation that may be applicable to the current one. Remind them how they <u>felt</u> in the past in a similar situation with difficult consequences. Never blame, shame, or make wrong. That just will not work. Bipolars are usually very prideful people which can be a blessing or a curse depending how they apply it in their lives. Show affinity, caring, concern, etc.
   Another intervention would be to sit down with the person when the person is clear thinking and decide what to do if an episode happens. You must have a leap-of-faith agreement with the person so they will take direction. You must be someone they trust. In one relationship between husband and wife, the husband agreed he would take medication for two months if his wife said so. That worked for them. If he didn't, he knew she would leave him. When manic, a person's judgement and conscience is diminished even though they may seem "brilliant", logically.
   You may notice that sometimes when a person is manic, they talk loudly. The voice volume control is in the prefrontal lobe. If the light is dimming in

the prefrontal lobe or out completely, they are not "seeing" themselves or "seeing" the environment. Hence the loudness.

Evolution

Did you ever hear of an "evolutionary psychologist"? I recently met one. They study evolution. I proposed the consideration that bipolar people may be nature's next evolution of man. She disagreed, but in the ensuing debate, I became more and more sure that bipolars are Mother Nature's next evolution. Some agree.

I don't mean to appeal to anyone's grandiosity, but I have known bipolars to be very creative, industrious, goal oriented, and think out of the box. They don't seem to need as much sleep as most people. They really do think faster than most people. They are driven when they have a goal to reach.

When I worked for IBM, I was given a temporary assignment to test the speed of a new piece of equipment. We couldn't find an impulse because it was so fast that our best test equipment wasn't fast enough to catch it. There was a lot of new equipment that went out to the field and had problems because it was too much for the peripheral devices. We had to make better peripheral devices. It was like putting a race engine in a Volkswagen bug. There were going to be problems. The Volkswagen bug was going to be all over the road. The tires would burn the rubber off. The clutch would burn out.

I have a friend who thinks about six times faster

than I do. He has a photographic memory. He gets along fine on six hours sleep. He is very decisive and his decisions hold up. He gets impatient with my slow speech and when I pause to think about my answers. I annoy him, even though he likes me. The only problem I can think of that he has is that his thoughts are so consuming that he doesn't have time to feel his feelings. If my mind operates as fast as a Pentium I computer, his is a Pentium VI. He remembers things that I would never remember like, "Jay, your tie clip was on crooked when you were here three months ago."

Research and Other Things

- There is some interesting research being done on the Transcranial Magnetic Stimulation. This is a magnetically charged device that is placed over the head and has shown some good results. There is no seizure associated with it or memory loss like with Electro- Convulsive Therapy (ECT).
- The NIMH (National Institute for Mental Health) is funded to research the bipolar disorder and has given grants around the country to universities for the purpose of researching family lines of bipolars.
- A possible gene has been identified for about ten percent of people with the bipolar disorder. This is good news, since the only way to diagnose, at this time, is to look at symptoms. A physical means of diagnosing would assist greatly. There have been other genes suspected of contributing to the bipolar disorder, but the new discovery is a definite gene. Undoubtedly, there are other genes involved giving to the various intensities and types of bipolar.

- The bipolar disorder gets misdiagnosed for OCD (Obsessive Compulsive Disorder), for example. Some people have obsessive thoughts ONLY when they are manic and they are given medication for OCD, which improperly treats the mania. Others get diagnosed schizophrenic or schizoaffective when they are actually just bipolar. Another common misdiagnosis is Intermittent Explosive Disorder (IED) for Bipolar. When a person is diagnosed with IED, the first thing I would do is to look for head traumas, thyroid, or adrenal gland problems to eliminate a physical possibility. Secondly, look for the possibility of physical abuse as a young child or pre-cognitively. If nothing is found, look for relatives who may be or may have been bipolar. If you find there is a genetic link (possibly undiagnosed) then the IED is probably a bipolar disorder.

- In some parts of the country, there has been success with thyroid medication (ie: Synthroid) to augment medication. It has been found that most people who are bipolar have a low, but normal, thyroid. When Synthroid is introduced, the bipolar medication can be lowered. Part of the research actually creates hyperthyroidism in bipolars and completely takes them off medication. The results of this research are not complete yet, but looks very promising. There doesn't seem to be the normally severe side effects for bipolars with the artificially induced hyperthyroidism.

"Lying"

This an interesting phenomenon that can test your ability to use your prefrontal lobe and discernment. For example, there was a ten year old (diagnosed bipolar) who called his mother a "blah blah" (I'll let you fill in the blanks.) She sent him up to his room to "get a new attitude". This was in the morning when he had his worst mood swings. Many bipolars seem to at their worse in the morning. The boy came back down ten minutes later and hugged his mother. She said, "Well, this is much better than calling me a blah blah." The child looked confused and said, "I didn't call you a blah blah!?" Mom said, "Why, you did too. Your father heard you say it. (She looks over at the father). Didn't you, dear." The father agreed with Mom. The boy looked very confused. It seemed that he didn't remember saying it. This boy was not a liar in general. He had owned up to doing things in the past. So what is the explanation?

Amphetamines affect the same dopamine centers as mania. People who have taken a lot of amphetamines will tell you that their memories are spotty or blank sometimes when they get high. I am sure you have heard of some people getting drunk and didn't remember dancing on the bar. (I am sure that has never happened to you, just "other" people.) When chemicals in the brain are poisoning the cognitive system, we don't remember things. He was in a different <u>state</u> of mind.

Have you ever been really angry, and the only memories you could conjure up were angry memories? A state of mind.

Speaking of state of mind, there is a difference between a feeling and a state of mind. A person can feel depressed and they will say, "I feel depressed again today. I hope it goes away soon." The state of mind of depression is when ...

everything seems bleak ... it seems that it always was bleak ... and it always will be bleak. This is a state of depression vs. a feeling of depression. A state of depression evokes a lack of hope.

There are some states of mind that are not cognitive states. Remember when you were one year old? I don't think so.

The Discovery channel followed a man through a drinking spree. The commentator said that each beer he drank eliminated 1000 years of evolution, so that after imbibing a case of beer, we can be fairly primitive without those executive functions. This "state of mind" depression may explain why there is so much suicide in the bipolars. It seems there is no hope.

The "uncognitive" state of mind that we get propelled into with substance abuse or chemical imbalance can account for memory lapses. Some alcoholics say they can't remember things they did, but after a few drinks, the memories start getting clearer. It almost like the brain has two separate time tracks.

After a manic episode, some people can't remember what they did. Part of this may be chemistry and part may be psychogenic amnesia. Psychogenic amnesia comes about when a person cannot confront something they may have done because it may have been way out of the range of their normal understanding of right and wrong.

Cognitive Behavioral Therapy

Research shows that cognitive behavioral therapy and educational therapy work for the bipolar disorder. That would make sense, in that they are temporarily very concrete. When the light bulb dims in the prefrontal lobe of the bipolar, she/he can only fall back on the operation of the "thinker" (concrete cognitive ability) to function. While most people can benefit from psychotherapy (insights), the Cognitive therapy specifically helps the bipolar for specifically the bipolar disorder. When the prefrontal lobe lights back up, again, insight therapy is good. The insight, judgment, and bigger picture fade in the throes of a manic episode.

The Spirit

My mother had a lot of spirit. Her body and brain could not accommodate it. She would constantly exhaust her body and her brain. She started to malfunction. Her mind and body became worn out from lack of sleep. She self medicated with alcohol, and pep pills (prescribed amphetamines). My uncle said about her once, "She has a lot of spirit, but not enough strength to carry it off."

I would re-phrase that and say, "She had a strong spirit, so much that her body and brain couldn't handle it"

My mother was a woman before her time. She organized a strike of farmer's wives in the 1940's. She was intelligent and articulate. I would catch her cleaning the kitchen floor at three AM in the morning. She loved animals and saved their lives. I remember once, my mother found three geese that couldn't fly due to being shot by hunters. She nursed them back to health over the winter and set them on our pond in the spring. In the fall they flew south but they came back in the spring with friends (20 or 30 more geese). As the years went on, there were eventually hundreds of geese on our pond and Mom wouldn't let anyone shoot them. She could be a pain to my father who was trying to run a farm (All that goose do-do).

The female side of my mother's family seemed to have "Nervous Breakdowns" (NBD's). My mother had an NBD before I was born and was given shock treatments while she was in the Navy. My grandmother had an NBD and was away for a year. I was told that there is an atypical bipolar disorder occurring on the female side, genetically. I don't know. All, I know is that they loved me and I loved them. My mother would try to answer all my questions. She spent time with me. She would always come up with something interesting and it was sometimes "out of the box". I could talk about anything with her. I had trouble understanding her mood swings and depression because there wasn't always something "out there" causing it. My mother had defects, but her gifts far outweighed them. She could get critical of me, but it rolled off my back because I knew for absolute certainty that I was special to her.

She was bipolar, surely loved me, and taught me to think out of the box. I wouldn't have traded her.

This book is updated every 1000 copies. If you have information or comments, please write to:
Dr. Jay Carter
P.O. Box 6048
Wyomissing, PA 19610
or at jaycarter115@cs.com
All mail will be read by Dr. Jay. You will be acknowledged for any information.

Suggested Readings:

An Unquiet Mind, by Kay Redfield Jamison
She is a psychologist who is bipolar.

Bipolar Disorder, by Francis Mark Mondimore,
M.D., John Hopkins University Press, 1999.
An excellent book on the bipolar disorder.

A Brilliant Madness; Living with Manic-Depression
Illness by Patty Duke
She is a well-known actress.

CABF.org
a good website for information about kids who are
bipolar. Good reference for physicians.

mhsource.com
a website for general information about the bipolar
disorder.

bipolarhappens.com
a website by someone who is not a therapist, but
has bipolar disorder and has found a way to deal
with it, even though she is allergic to some of the
medication.

"Young and Bipolar", Time Magazine, August 19,
2002. An excellent article. It came out after this
book and verified the validity by consensus.

The Bipolar Child by Janice and Demitri Papolos,
M.D.

Bibliography

This book was phenomenologically created out of the experience of the author and other sources including:

- Feedback from psychiatrists, medical doctors, psychologists, social workers, and counselors, across the country at my Bipolar Seminars. (thousands of people who are right there working with bipolar every day).

- Two and a half years at Berks County Prison (as a staff member, of course)

- Over five years at the Caron Foundation doing psychological evaluations.

- Personal experience living with family members.

- One years experience doing psychological evaluations for high risk children in the Wraparound Program.

- Doing business consulting with bipolar clients.

- Personal friendships with people who are bipolar.

Dr. Carter gives seminars on the Bipolar Disorder, Anger Management, Executive Functions for Business, and other subjects. You may contact him at:
Unicorn Press, P.O. Box 6048
Wyomissing, PA 19610
or at JayCarter115@CS.COM.
***THIS BOOK AND OTHERS CAN BE PURCHASED ON** www.jaycarter.net*